The Method

Rob Stanton was born in County Durham, raised in the Midlands, and educated in Cardiff and Leeds. Rob now lives in the U.S. with wife, daughter and cats. His poems and critical works have appeared in numerous online and print publications. *The Method* is his first book.

The Method

Rob Stanton

Penned in the Margins

LONDON

PUBLISHED BY PENNED IN THE MARGINS
53 Arcadia Court, 45 Old Castle Street, London E1 7NY
www.pennedinthemargins.co.uk

The right of Rob Stanton to be identified as the author of this work has been asserted
by him in accordance with Section 77 of the Copyright, Designs and Patent Act 1988.

First published 2011

Printed in the United Kingdom by MPG Biddles Ltd.

ISBN
978-0-9565467-6-0

Acknowledgements

The following poems have appeared in the following publications, sometimes in different (and sometimes in radically different) forms:

'The Account' (as 'I I I') in *Shearsman*.
'Tuymans Sonnets 9 & 10' in *The Rialto*.
'Ode: on Arrival', 'Ode: On Sampling (i)', 'Ode: On Sampling (ii)' and 'Ode: On the Recent Spate of Obituaries' in *Jacket*.

Many thanks to Tony Frazer, Michael Mackmin, Pam Brown and John Tranter for their support.

For Kamille

CONTENTS

The Method

Of what is this house composed if not of the sun

Wallace Stevens

I

The Account

The Account

First person singular? Adam? But he
lost it. Eve? She
swam the channel

*

Yr movements telegraph 'Liberty'
to space. The
Great Wall

*

Foundations
eye
the apex

Ode: On Arrival

Same yellow jacket (white & black-specked trim), same air of total involvement in distraction (in being distracted), same way of hovering in the whole trained light of another's active will? Check. This one, however, notices you; you double-take. Action proves nothing (us: our entrances, our activities, environment). A gesture arrested in bloom, transitory, permanent – an atmosphere turned amber, pinning down. (Drowned or blissful, taking her place?) I could (*eclipse and cloud it with a wink*) bow down. Threshold gains: a passive onslaught not (as heretofore) a balanced interrogation, lit & under siege. Precocious, precious enfant – ancient, lapidary – is delight her get-out clause? Her destination? Out of the question. An aching suspicion, beside the point, surely, mere anxiety, that something so complete (anything so) does not need witnesses.

Face

Narrative continues
into sleep.

*Fire does
destroy everything.*

[…]

Everything deepens
into distance.

Extending a
deictic hand.

Away

I keep
not identifying.

Sumptuous clothing
in abeyance.

[…]

Hold throat
into tune.

*Traffic islands
island traffic.*

From

No escape
from energy.

(A far
flung matter.)

[...]

Castle ramparts
riding roughshod.

Object you
yourself made.

Them

Take finger
off pulse.

Shatter proof
window open.

[...]

Gather them
before opening.

Reproductions sink
or swim.

Ode: On Sampling (i)

Crickets' song harangues the interloper, sets him down. Flowers differently here. More snail, less speed. Tease out that total moment, let it spin. Held hand over eyes and brows, cool earth; see intimacy hear. A little hold off, pause for breath, perspective. Taken, jerky, to the next edited adventure. A chase after abandon, coming close. Panting not breathing – a moment after echoes, is extended. *I'm happy I'm happier*. A scarcely seen declension of pines round an everyday pond no call for hope. Spring, after all, is.

Some

Get off
next stop.

Couple of
unnotable days.

[...]

Same white
bloody pigeon.

Split pie
five ways.

Many

If it
please you.

Even in
Arcadia, I.

[...]

Odd, the
hawthorn's coverage.

Stimulate it
toward issue.

Made

The dead
owe us.

All trains
serve Paris.

[...]

A hand
made technology.

We stick
to paths.

Same

A hand
written invitation.

Some detachment
harbours intent.

[...]

Onus placed
on privacy.

Branches surge
and meet.

Ode: On the Recent Spate of Obituaries

Noon (& so on). (Do you *want* to end up surrounded by doctors & nurses? *I want out.* Less an essay, more a gesture. More? I am less; not cut out for survival.) Does a lack of aversion to busses indicate a willingness to wait, to be jostled, cramped, to endure frustration indefinitely? On day-long, night-long repeat: the AC's sudden outburst, periodic – a static industrial surrounding environment – long-lost, far-fetched, missing in action. Dust motes metaphor. A cigarette as soul-exhaust (what happens if I don't?). I spent the world's luck being here. A good look over the long graves.

The Insider

Canny wee thing, in
& out, where are you
headed to now, so
puling, knock-kneed, weak?
Where's the fun in that?

II

The Tuymans Sonnets

*Yet the absence of the imagination had
Itself to be imagined*

Wallace Stevens

The light. Its dimness. Its yellowness.

Samuel Beckett

A sea. 'The meaning
behind the allegorical title
is the intention
to attach

a second
non-existent picture
to the picture
like

an association
or collage.' 'A picture [...] like *Gaskamer* is,
solely because of [its] title, a

superimposed designation, a deeper
sense, a kind
of metonym.' A prow.

I

1. *Arena*, 1978.

'Annihilation, hygiene, consumerism, production &
propaganda.' For starters. Losers, glued
with paint. *Cool loners. Pinups. Pimps.* Our muddy, troubled
    personages. (Our
problem with sincerity: see: performance on performance: see:

the staging. Semi-permeable glad-rags meant
for business. The indiscretion of the soul's existence. 'A
constant uneasiness like a
constant [music].' Noise

we have no hope
of escaping. 'Sentinel's horn
sounds so homely from his tower, his voice invites

so hospitably.') A gift exchange
'aids those it aids'. Phone it in, in
step with what elapses.

2. *Arena*, 1978.

A martyrology
in bikinis. Beheld by,
beholden to, the severed
real. Their auras

triumphant. Not
in a recess, but floating
up. Toward the
onlooker (& all his charm).

This universe will
kill a man. Talked
through the show, stood

up before the final
act: momentum. Curtain
calls not promised/promising.

3. *Hands*, 1978 & *Nr.6*, 1978.

Desiring machine, faux-complicated.
Enigma an affront. Some monster
from a Doctor Who episode, all stocky-
cosmic, hands held out to us, as though we,

by looking, could find fingers
for them all (face pasted on later, an after-
thought). Picked-at raw nerve, thought-
lessly repeated; Arctic survivor, wrapped up

against the worst to come. (Mask might be
enticing, a false hope.) Sky, sea
shroud. A bigger move, a smaller

room, grin pulled back, a few
stray hairs an accident.
Psychology *is* biology, for the most part.

4. *Amnesia*, 1980.

Repression
reconstitutes
you. You choose
to take in

the proffered landscape
– 'painterly': some water, trees, old house, another
watermill – & so
the oval darkens, spelling out

its real name. Meaning
held for you is not
the point:

we
see your evasion; it
is ours.

5. *The Correspondence*, 1985.

'Arousing a sense of agreeable
restfulness': feeling secured: 'a
constant pressure via constant homesickness'. Flat
depth. Stuffed fear. Sorrow of getting

to know someone – anyone! – an un-
alien opposite who should hide
another (pincer pattern wallpaper; head-
on perspective dominating scale). Cross

equals drama: red paint marks
the spot; diminishment-as-given. 'There
is always […] a weak spot […] or hole […] through which

you enter.' Eyes final wall. The background-foreground
ebbing in, flows out; is reckless. Four
chairs round the table signal concord.

6.

'Without violence
there is no visual realm.
Without the idea of
opening something up

there is no boundary.
I would not interpret it
on a moral level, however.'
On a sponsored level, maybe?

'Indifference is also a form
of violence, as are
omission and re-

production. Violence is
for me mainly an
atmospheric picture.' Yes. No.

7.

Act differently. Sort of antique. Sort of
vacuous (sit in a pool of colour, pool
yourself, mouth the bitten apple or
a stop-cock). Cut-out eye. The element

of [someone]'s use of objects in a portrait, a
'blindfold space of mirrors'. 'For me
it is important to be able to see
that limit.' 'The beginning is always more

difficult to name.' He begs to rend-
er detail. 'An aperture must first
be found.' Adds little to production, a

black name. Uncle to deception. Leave out
that middle part. 'Live with yr family
forever, and be a failure.'

8.

A version of himself. A halo
I think. Matriculated self. Echo.
Echo. (His dreams are not
available to us.) 'Entire exhibitions

could be present on
one single sheet.' I hesitate
to think. 'Everyone has
his own handwriting anyway.' 'My

interest has been the amazing opening in the drawing and how
to increase it even further.' Drawing a blank. 'In
tiny drawings one can avoid losing oneself

in the position one finds oneself
in.' Singularly wounding. 'I
destroy a lot.' Incorporates my whole.

9.

Two cameras face this way. A third
faces into them. Cars supply domestic
space. A 'tiny' space. Sound sucked out. Small & slightly
sad. Villas, ghostly rooms, enclosures, average out, an

anthology. The melancholy notes identify
strain (assumed mastery appropriate, an
apple memento). Clowns. Flags. Toys. Detached
eyeballs (dimensions do not indicate

egress). Other, more recent smudges. 'A track
which cries out to be taken up and blurred.' 'At
[its] beginning [...] drawing was more autonomous.' 'More

secret, more blurred.' Burned images of burning. The most
basic, more or less. Seeing it, then reaching down
to pick it up. Us seeing that. And looking down.

10.

A plan to plan. To execute. To sketch an exit
in. Quickness equals precision. ('Paper has [already]
its own history.') Gesture, expression, circum-
scribed. Page-as-scenery, formal, found. Collision.

Collusion. That ominous cross. That glasses
maketh the man. Hand & eye. 'Something sick'
depicted. Picketed. 'Drawings are there
like a gap; they are convincing': '[a] good [one] should

omit a lot'. Indelible. Inedible. 'What *should* we do
about what we do?' Functionality revealed. Support
revealed. Hopeless focus, masked-as-lake. 'Not as

compulsive as [...] painting' but '[p]aradoxically [...] despite
being quick [they] continue further and further.'
Negatives. Edges. Contours. Passages.

11. *Antichamber*, 1985.

Commerce of voices
– on radio, tape, disc –
replacing memory (archives no such
sorry repositories here). A slow quick slow

of pencil dash turned
painted stroke: a spider-architecture
(nexus, web, speed-built, intriguing, taking
our attention hostage) replicates a motion

in, out: a frantic will
lagging after thought-speed, scrawling, crawls
thru three dimensions, grapples with

the higher functions, making
monsters out of texture
& air. . . .

12. *Encounter, 1985.*

Coming
round the corner to
be storyboarded. Giant squiggle a scrunched-up
piece of paper, a drawing discarded, an obstacle given

a wide berth. A cartoon
man – E.T. – peeks out sheepishly, scouting ahead. He plans
to go
right round. Is he

'interested in pictures that
[do not] visualize anything
that actually existed'? He is

concerned with
A to B. He
plans to go right round.

13.   *Eight*, 1986.

Intense effort
– passed off
as childish –
marks infinity.

'[S]enseless' (apparently). No. Not
quite. Two tramlines
track a
linear concept through the snow, a truer hypothesis. Still,

we want
the pattern, the
orchestrated intersection –

'pulled off
for a lark' –
a limited time only.

14.   *Gaskamer*, 1986.

A *warm painting*
of *something horrific.* A product
of immense boredom. One shadow
seeps away

into a
drain. *Its duration*
is inhuman. (How long could you
sit before it? Without a break?) Convincing because

inaccessible, flattened. A
stab at
existence. A

reduction to dots, or not
quite. One shadow stays
extant.

15. *Gaskamer*, 1986.

Sunken, somehow
sun-filled, memorably lit.
Meaning
more than image; light

an insidious, insistent evil.
Dark presents itself – a ruse – as exit.
Our expectation thwarted: what
do these things do? Most

interior
beauty
untenable. This sun

will not
go down
a thousand years.

16. *Schwarzheide*, 1986.

You
only paint
what's there,
not what

is not: the
camp
has been
removed,

you paint
the trees;
the trees

have been
removed, you
paint the paint.

17. *Our New Quarters*, 1986.

'Quarters' endlessly
divisible, dispossessing, until you stand,
crowded, on a pinhead. Why
English? For the difference's sake? As lingua franca? Coincidence?
   (No: we know; we knew.) So why

the incongruous
postcard jauntiness? A set-up for the pre-
judgemental onlooker? We
are quite at home.

One wonders.
Each apartment
a cave-mouth, chipped

into rock, a fleeting
shelter. One jaundiced tree
'resembles' a crack.

18. *Hotel Room*, 1987.

The
room resembles
itself; it re-
assembles

itself – as we, as guest,
are superseded. A wish
to be remembered
to transcend. A late

twentieth century
version
of same. You

are not
your surround. You are
not not your surround.

19. *Writing,* 1988.

I am told
what to write.
I am
the riot-barrier.

The text falters. The
background is metallic. The panicked
line
mainlines, railroaded. You want to 'pull

the medium out
of its graphic
rigidity'? Right

to name
nothing
you negotiate.

20. *Child Abuse*, 1989.

'Advertising [the] void.' Much worse: a
corrupted space a pristine sandbox (green
& yellow innocence) overlaid by
featureless icon, gap

awaiting price. '[The] idea
of rape.' Colour stimulus drives a reaching
out. 'Even I
was shocked by

the result.' Over the
milky horizon a 'great
distance arose', no actual

violation. Instead, an agenda
tattooed
into.

21.   *Die Weidergutmakung*, 1989.

Humiliation over
proper envoys – hands, eyes
cut off, isolate (grid has been imposed and is
a whim). Tax-deductible blueprint identity jelly-

like up close; the colour coloured in is just
not plausible. As quality *is*
quantity, parasites exemplars, tokens, subject
is object

forever & ever
amen. Formation clapping is
the point: be people people want

to photograph. Adopt an
apocalyptic acceptance. Re-
cord, -coil, -call.

22. *The Cry*, 1989 & *The Murderer*, 1989.

Need a good cry. Or
to escape (down backstairs or
past glass, one solitary window-box a flash of
red & green): a number

of steps down, arms
held out at an angle, suspicious, blunt but
not without purpose – hat coat pants organic
green & brown. The

tie noose
dress bright the
hand a

mobile shadow
brought to bear the sun
accomplice shadow sanctuary.

23. *Suspended*, 1989.

Something like
something else: a
point of comparison.
Like seeing this

particular painting (its static actors, frantic charge, plot, props,
    some synthesis) as it
carries
a narrative
through the point

of no return. Like traffic
on the weekend. Like living
in the past and refusing

to care. Like liking
the likely
story better. . . .

24.   *Suspended,* 1989 & *The Swimming Pool,* 1989.

Desire to
possess them
breathlessly confessed:
'[i]f a toy falls it

will break.'
Fun & games
suspended –
for our pleasure –

in the gene-pool. Areas
of foliage, greyness
beyond; a house

all homely-shady, not at all
substantial. ('This is
[a] problem [that has been dealt with] from another point of view
    elsewhere.')

25. *Secrets*, 1990.

Do closed eyes
hold the whole
man in? He wants
to be unknowable, for us

to notice. His over-
compensation, then, is pointless.
Composure of the grave, of grave
attire, demeanour, will not cover up

the vision of a boy allowed to play.
His black neck-tie will drag him into sleep.
Flat angles, planes: he's dreaming

up a building.
What's under all those lids? A dome so vast
it rains indoors?

26. *Body*, 1990.

Not –
apparently –
a person *or*
a doll. It's

where you enter, zip up the zip behind you, become
whole again. Injured identity not
the point; the point
a necessary wound mid-torso (looks

like it goes
right round
the back) where stuffing, apparently, can be added

'to make
it alive [or]
more alive'. 'Votive' not the word, yet is.

27. *Disenchantment*, 1990.

Total icon, to be
prayed to. A systematic
warding off; a breaking
of a spell. Magically asleep

electron, neutron, in
the atom: sperm-child
approaching
mother-egg, in rings.

Attraction?
Repulsion?
Awake

in ambiguity
& doubt, I want to say
I don't know.

28. *Hotel Lobby*, 1991.

A friendly face
bulges to one side. A
bigger place
eats us up.

Guard-rails
evaporate; light fixtures dis-
solute & scratchy.
Where's my drink,

my antidote?
Steps down don't help anything.
We find ourselves

the spot
we had
forgotten.

29. *Silence*, 1991.

Total ghost (not quite
centre-stage: to the
left, slightly; nearer
the top). Orange-yellow-green under

the eyes; the eyes
alive, yet shut. The oblong mouth.
One nostril white. One nostril black.
(Vacuuming in

extraneous life.)
The child, the
child's parents, we

are there. The softest
[sigh/moan/gasp]
escapes, breaking the title.

30. *Ice*, 1992.

This – our body –
everywhere
denied. The locked door, handle
out, light along

its stolid bar, the lock beneath, abstracted
eye, entrance
or exit.
Glove, all comic-

puffy, hanging
dead weight. Finally: tray
in close up, slabs of ice, two

taken out, presented, touching.
On ice, the
saying goes.

Der Diagnostiche Blick
(The Diagnostic Gaze)

31.

Parthenogenesis. 'Nature itself' prone
& puppy-like. The promised drama
has not happened: the pin-
up legends telescope

to tautness. ('By
economy
I mean[t]
the idea

of sharpness.')
Not with intention.
Not within tension.

Nature sad
and getting
sadder.

32.

Nebulous emotions cauterised. Pleasure is there
'in the making'. Prepare
the soul (or salad) for
some torture.

(What health
looks like. So much
less frontal. Anaemic. Our own
best product

foiled & packaged tightly.) 'Type
of arousal.' What
will all

these gazes do
in time?
Settle?

33.

First view: a man aloof who
doesn't know it. Second: shifty. Smudged black ink, shiny
with moisture the painting
doesn't actually hold. Mere accidents of clothing and

arrival 'mak[e] the eye
look askance'. Doctors' murmurs lean
to silence. The quiet of a waiting room
or morgue. Quite science-abstract, wholly

visible, he'll never have
'a definite face'
to look from; rumour and all vagueness

will attend him, freshly mounted rancid
wan crybaby (some final proof he has
two lungs and breathes).

34.

Adorno: 'It is arrogant and almost
contemptuous towards the victims
to talk like them, as though one
were one

of them'. Put
through the wash
too many times. Not
that much

brighter, vivid, than the walls. The
walls, themselves, not much in evidence. An
ever-present frown

as lack
of disclosure. Identity-as-disease. Illness
as a pretext. Self 'only ever [as] punctuation'.

35.

Mouth – scar – an
entry-
point, obscene: dull lips
drawn in; eyes, dull, thrown back;

nose tapering
to a right
angle: supreme magnetic presence
of our time: smug levels of content in our dis-

ease (ears bat-like,
Nosferatu-lite); 'some
"scepticism"

about material' good: a
sudden close-up shows some
spots and motes.

36.

Fetishise
what's wrong. Make
masks trans-
ferable. (A

softer stance
in ever-
harder bonds.) When
'you find you

can edit anything'
edit nothing. Face for-
ever calm, just not upset: bold,

ever-startled speculation, etiolated, ill: *it
has no veins no heart no
pulse no no.*

37.

Old-age reproduction of the first
dud offering. What
is wrong here? What
is not? 'I

wish to avoid
[cultivating] a style or
expressive approach
at all costs.' I

alone. The task
only begun & time's
been called. I

obstacle, obstruction. 'Most eyes
in medical books look
straight into the lens; I changed that.'

38.

Another, and another, and another
quirk of pain, non-toxic and illuminating
here. Compromises, life: the seeing of a doctor
necessary. 'Project yr own

physicality
upon the image.' Don't.
Float in airy
thoughtfulness

above. . . .
Full-blooded hyper-lips all life
drained to, their residue a slime . . . despair not

touched on yet . . . a simple case. . . . 'I'm
afraid I
just don't care.'

39.

Too little thought of: what the limbs
resist, the bare contagious manning
of the lifeboats (all false hope in fast escape
discretely scuppered). Skippered well, the vessel

drifts abandoned, *Marie Celeste*
of wistfulness, allure. The artist
parts the waters
with a paintbrush. Here, there, abs-

traction rears
its ugly head, highlights the thought's original
malaise. 'The face

the soul', it seems to state. Unearthed: a fix. (The brain
pities the body, is
the body.)

40.

Body lies down. Nature,
its superior, vacillates. Words, wounded,
in a wall
of flesh: an image

too (?) divorced
from human context:
objects . . . orbits . . . universes . . . static.
Sickness sickness,

not a progress. Incompleteness
is their final form ('as if erased,
cancelled'). What could (or would) they

say (or cry)? Infectious
silence, billboard apparition. '[B]eing
far more visible.' What? 'Far more [un]sound.'

III

The Method

The Method

We'll never know that unbelievable
head, those outstanding eyes. The trunk
stills shines, but more like a subdued candelabrum
reflecting on its own reluctant – if

staggering – power. Why else would we
be riveted to that impressive chest? Why else
notice that chuckle spread down tensing abs
to a barely-there but still productive groin?

Take that and all you're left with is a slab
of mutilated stone – defeated, slumped – not
glistening like a predator's subtle fur, nor

diffusing light of stars' intensity. There's
not a single part of it that does not
see your life. You must change.

Ode: On Developing Character

Sophrosyne versus nosos, thin management. The egret's tense, terse neck, beak – a record player's stylus – drops – all taut aggression, skill, feint – & comes up with nothing. A family slips into plastic tubes & drifts down the river into town, spinning slowly. Many roads & no acceleration. My hand hurts something dreadful. (Moved to read 'Resolution and Independence' over once again.) During the (mildly) drug-induced sleep, your primary character (a dumpy woman herself the subject of drug trials) cannot keep herself awake, one dissolute moment separate from the next, her adopted child safe from creeping persecution at the art gallery. *Home is where your harmer is, your hammer is.* Cop interrogates Marion Crane (is right to: she has the money), exuding menace, mirror-shaded. Shorn of line, character is forced to shine elsewhere, is sentenced. Work backwards from the words: imagine a speaker who could say them unexpectedly and unrehearsed. Trust no-one who says they have seen you asleep.

Sift

Mill-pool evaporates
every summer.

[...]

Need its
better cousin.

Want the
sun rising.

*Jackdaw in
his tree.*

Want

*Little bits
of tinsel.*

[...]

Drift down
into enclosure.

An ocean
of recrimination.

Slap that
sentence down.

Into

Nobody holds
a match.

*Just the
delivery system.*

[…]

Gun in
yr face.

Keys in
the ignition.

Bits

"Just saying
is all."

Acrobat more
than *diplomat*.

[…]

*I mean
I hope.*

A feather
touch down.

Ode: On Sampling (ii)

Lawns laws accomplish. Autumn flags: less haze, more definition. Drained armature of asking. Watching, over hours, as dawn arrived. Less & less, this valley of time between expenditures. Two shuffled contexts speak, & spark, each revolution. Mechanics skim an inner menagerie. Slept so thin, the dream seemed firm assessment, piercing through. Pressed into not returning. *Can't, as parasite, differentiate.* Dog seen from bus, on the tip of the season's tongue. Sojourns between departure lounges.

Walk

Here's what
isn't there.

Eyes turn
to tools.

[...]

The focal
points beyond.

Submit to
'reasonable' force.

Over

Existence as
an affront.

The whole
world rhymes.

[...]

Is this
epistle overbearing?

Mother bears
the brunt.

Aery

Edifice marked
by lyric.

Is such
deportment realistic?

[…]

Such an
empty house.

And he
went in.

Bays

Memoirs of
a joke.

Surprise at
its extremity.

[…]

Pen hung
from indecision.

"I'll be
signposting forever."

Ode: To Ideal Fire

A 'sun-loving herb'. One thousand thousand things drawn taut. A secret kink of thought no matter. . . . *Blinding* as appreciation, praise. (Upside down hubris turned inside out, epidermis stripped, dermis stripped, the depths revealed, a film of blood all over the trees, a piercing shriek shearing away.) *I wanna be machine.* Our singing mine. (Even our discords scurry into place; folded in; secured.) *&* *they to heaven* (gods themselves bury your victims, victor). So, why not turn your blowtorch onto this? See, but have no witnesses. See arrow exit wound, flesh instantly heal, bow-strings go limp, antagonists drift from the field, their argument forgotten.

The Wait

Bureaucracy is my
friend

      as Lazarus (pulled
up sharp)

        kept
pecking.

Notes

I

'Ode: On Arrival'. Inspired by various paintings by Jan Vermeer: *Women with a Lute* (1663-64 or 1662-63), *Women with a Pearl Necklace* (1662-64), *A Lady Writing a Letter* (1665-66), *Mistress and Maid* (1667-68), *The Love Letter* (1669-70) and *The Guitar Player* (1672).

'The Insider'. Somewhat after Hadrian's 'Animula, vagula, blandula'. Apologies to both poet and original for liberties taken.

II

The 'sonnets' in this sequence respond to the art and thought of Belgian painter Luc Tuymans (1958 -). Where individual poems refer to particular works by Tuymans, I have indicated this in their titles. A few further notes are necessary:

7- 10. These four sonnets refer to a variety of Tuymans' preliminary sketches & watercolours, as reproduced in Berg, Bitterli & Pirotte, *Luc Tuymans: The Arena*.

31-40. These sonnets relate to a series of ten paintings from 1992, based on case photographs Tuymans found in various medical textbooks.

I am indebted to the following publications:

Stephan Berg, Konrad Bitterli and Philippe Pirotte, *Luc Tuymans: The Arena* (Ostfildern: Hatje Cantz Verlag, 2003).

Jan Hoet, Philippe Pirotte and Robert Storr, *Luc Tuymans: Mwana Kitoko (Beautiful White Man)* (Ghent: Stedelijk Museum voor Actuele Kunst, 2001).

Ulrich Loock, Juan Vicente Aliaga, Nancy Spector and Hans Rudolf Reust, *Luc Tuymans*, 2nd ed. (London: Phaidon, 2003).

Gerrite Vermeiren, *Luc Tuymans: I don't get it* (Ghent: Ludin, 2007).

III

'The Method'. Somewhat after Rilke's 'Archaïscher Torso Apollos'. Apologies, again, to both poet and original.